Hazel King

Trends in Textile Technology

DYES AND DECORATION

REVISED AND UPDATED

Heinemann
LIBRARY

www.heinemann.co.uk/library
Visit our website to find out more information about Heinemann Library books.

To order:
☎ Phone 44 (0) 1865 888066
▤ Send a fax to 44 (0)1865 314091
▭ Visit the Heinemann Library Bookshop at www.heinemann.co.uk/library to browse our catalogue and order online.

First published in Great Britain by Heinemann Library, Halley Court, Jordan Hill, Oxford OX2 8EJ, part of Harcourt Education.
Heinemann Library is a registered trademark of Harcourt Education Ltd.

© Harcourt Education Ltd 2008
The moral right of the proprietor has been asserted.

Editorial: Sarah Shannon
Design: Philippa Jenkins
Picture Research: Hannah Taylor
Production: Duncan Gilbert

Originated by Chroma Graphics
Printed and bound in China by Leo Paper Group

ISBN 978 0 431 99017 0
12 11 10 09 08
10 9 8 7 6 5 4 3 2 1

British Library Cataloguing in Publication Data
King, Hazel
    Dyes and Decoration. - 2ed.
    - (Trends in textile technology)
    1. Dyes and dyeing - Juvenile literature
    2. Colour in the textile industry - Juvenile literature
    667.3
A full catalogue record for this book is available from the British Library.

Acknowledgements
The publishers would like to thank the following for permission to reproduce photographs: ©Anne Griffiths pp.**32**, **33** (www.pocketmouse.co.uk); ©Bridgeman Art Library p.**36** (Burghley House Collection); ©Corbis pp.**9**, **22**, **27** (Reuters); ©Eric Pelham p.**43**; ©Eye Ubiquitous p.**18**; ©Getty Images p.**21** (Robert Harding World Imagery); ©Harcourt Education Ltd. p.**15** (Tudor Photography); ©H Rogers p.**43**; ©Harcourt Education Ltd. pp.**11**, **13**, **17**, **25**, **29**, **30**, **31**, **38**, **40** (G Boden); ©Jennie Zipperer, The Embellished Cloth, 2705 Millstone Plantation Road, Tallahassee, FL 32312: *embellishedcloth.com* p.**35**; ©Novara Group p.**10**; ©Trip p.**4** (M Ewing), **37** (Chris Parker), ©Streano p.**43** (Havens).

Cover photograph of a close up of embroidery work reproduced with permission of Alamy Images/Westend61.

Our thanks to Carey Clarkson for her assistance during the preparation of this book.

Every effort has been made to contact copyright holders of any material reproduced in this book. Any omissions will be rectified in subsequent printings if notice is given to the publishers.

Disclaimer
All the Internet addresses (URLs) given in this book were valid at the time of going to press. However, due to the dynamic nature of the Internet, some addresses may have changed, or sites may have changed or ceased to exist since publication. While the author and publishers regret any inconvenience this may cause readers, no responsibility for any such changes can be accepted by either the author or publishers.

Any words appearing in the text in bold, **like this**, are explained in the Glossary.

Contents

Colour, wonderful colour

Colour can inspire. Colour can influence. Colour can have a huge impact on all our lives. Consider for a moment some aspects of life that are affected by colour – traffic lights, uniforms, football strips, skin colour, food, flags, make-up, funerals, weddings... the list goes on.

Searching for something new to wear gives a good insight into the importance of colour in textiles. If you are browsing through shops it is likely that you will first pick up an item of clothing because you are attracted to the colour, before you consider its style or size. Of course, the effect of colour is not limited to clothing. You can give a room a cosy feel or a chilly effect just by changing the colour scheme. Brochures used for choosing paint illustrate this really well, as they often show examples of rooms decorated using various shades of colour (also known as **hues**).

Colour choice

Colour can sometimes help in creating a particular effect. The look of an interior design is affected by the furniture, by how it is positioned, and by the furnishings and fabrics as well as by other items in the room. In addition to colour, clothes can provide a particular effect by the choice and cut of fabric, any accessories or **embellishments** and, of course, the person wearing the outfit.

Colours change according to fashion, and fashion reflects the values of the society for any given period of time. Today our society is concerned with environmental issues and this is quite evident in some of our fashions. Many people want natural colours to go with their preference for natural fibres and fabrics. In contrast, the celebrations for the millennium seem set to continue for some time in fashion terms, as clothes become bold and bright, with lots of orange and plenty of clashing colour.

Seeing the light

Light plays a crucial role in our ability to see colours. It sounds obvious to say we can see colour only when light is available, but the light from the sun actually contains all colours – so, where there is no light, there is no colour. As sunlight passes through raindrops, a rainbow is formed because the light is split up, enabing us to see the main colours of the spectrum.

As sunlight passes through raindrops, a rainbow is formed.

The spectrum is visible light divided into all the colours. The colours are red, orange, yellow, green, blue, indigo and violet.

Absorbing colours

When light falls on an object certain colours of the spectrum are absorbed and others are reflected. The colours we see are those that are reflected by the object. For example, if someone enters the room wearing a blue wig, we know it is blue because the wig is absorbing all the light (containing all colours of the spectrum) except blue, which is reflected back for us to see. If, however, the wig had been white then all the colours of the spectrum would have been reflected. Black, on the other hand, is seen as black because it absorbs all the colours in the spectrum of light, and none is reflected back.

Colour characteristics

All colours have two main characteristics. They have a value, which is a measure of their lightness or darkness, and they have an intensity, which indicates the strength of the colour. By adding white to a colour you create a **tint**, and by adding black you produce a **shade**.

A wheel of colour

The colour wheel is a way of representing colours. The colours are divided into three types: primary, secondary and tertiary.
- **Primary** colours are red, yellow and blue.
- **Secondary** colours are orange, green and violet, and are made by mixing two primary colours together. For example, mix red and yellow and create orange.

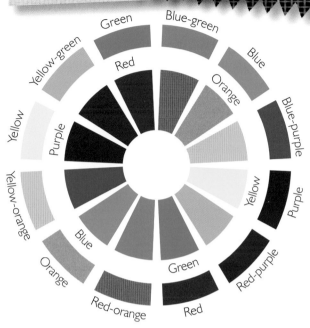

The colours are divided into three types: primary, secondary and tertiary.

- **Tertiary** colours are a mix of a primary and a secondary colour. So, red (primary) may be mixed with orange (secondary) to produce an orange red, and so on.

Properties of Colour – Value

Value is a term used to describe the lightness or darkness of a colour. Lighter versions of a colour are said to have higher values, and darker versions, lower values. Value is an important characteristic of colour for fashion drawing – a garment with a lot of drape and deep folds will show a range of colour values, from high colour values on the flat surfaces to the lowest value of the colour in the deepest recesses. Different colours have different intrinsic value levels – yellow is light, higher in value than blue, which is a dark colour. The interaction of colours is highly relevant in fashion drawing and so it is important to have a sound understanding of colour combinations and to make effective and coherent choices about the colours used.

Changing colours

We take it for granted that our clothes and other textile items come in such a wonderful array of colours. But this is possible only when a **dye** is added. A dye is a substance that is added to textiles in order to give them colour. Originally people dyed **yarns** and fabrics with natural dyes such as plant leaves and berries. Then, during the 1850s, a scientist called William H. Perkins discovered **synthetic** dyes, and a whole new world of bright and bold colours was unleashed.

Colourfastness

Dyes work by absorbing some of the light that hits the fabric and reflecting back the colour that is seen. They can be applied to the fibre, the yarn or the fabric, and usually this is done using either cold or hot water. However, dyes would not be much use unless they could be made to be fast, or **colourfast**. This means that they will not wash out or rub off. Sometimes colours do fade over time, but this effect may be desired, for example, with denim jeans.

Mordants

In order to make a dye colourfast, a **mordant** is added during the dyeing process. A mordant is a chemical that can 'fix' the dye so it will not wash out or fade. The various different types of **dyestuffs** require different types of mordant, but the most usual ones are alum, tin, chrome and iron. Some mordants can be toxic to use, so people working with them must take great care.

Natural dyes

Like weaving and spinning, natural dyeing is a very old craft. Natural dyes produce 'countryside' shades. These are muted colours that tone easily with one another. Natural dyeing has a very 'green' environmentally-friendly image. Not only does it produce natural hues (colours), it can also involve recycling by using onion skins or carrot tops to dye fabric, instead of throwing them away!

The first colours that were used for dyeing were acquired from animal and vegetable sources. Sepia brown was obtained from

Natural designers!

It is important that manufacturers and designers work together to protect the environment.

Paul Smith has introduced an 'Ecollection' into his fashion chain which involves the use of a special dyeing process that reduces waste products as well as using less water and energy.

Another solution is to use naturally coloured fibres or 'colour grown' fibres; an idea pursued by Sally Fox, who is the sole producer of a naturally coloured cotton with a fibre length long enough to mill. The product known as Foxfibre comes in shades of green, brown, beige and blue and is grown organically.

cuttlefish, while some mosses and lichens can provided green colours. The South American beetle is a source for cochineal pink, and flowers such as saffron and marigold can be used to supply yellows and golds. Bark called logwood bark can produce different shades of brown and black. Some natural dyestuffs and the colours that they produce are shown in the table to the right.

Indigo blue

During Roman times, the woad plant (*Isatis tinctoria*) was used to produce the colour indigo, which is a shade of blue. At one time it was the most important crop in central Europe and today it is making a comeback in England!

The Ministry of Agriculture and some companies are running a research project into the development of a new crop of woad. This will be used to produce natural indigo much more quickly that it usually takes. Traditionally the extraction process for woad took twelve weeks, but now the time taken from harvesting the crop to producing a blue dye takes just twelve minutes.

Natural indigo is usually used to dye denim. At the moment, most of this natural dye is supplied to Britain from India and China.

Yellows/golds
Marigold
Onion skins
Stinging nettles
Lily of the valley leaves
Fawns/beiges
Dock leaves
Heather
Lichen
Pine cones, crushed
Browns
Walnut shells, crushed and soaked
Elder leaves
Dock leaves
Blues/purples/mauves
Blackberries
Elderberries
Marjoram flower buds
Sloe berries
Blueberries
Reds/pinks
Madder roots
Sorrel roots
Red cabbage leaves
Greens
Apples bark
Bracken
Privet leaves
Tomato leaves and stems

Industrial dyes and dyeing

Industrial dyeing generally involves the use of synthetic dyes which, unlike natural dyes, can produce strong, intense colours. The other main reasons for using synthetic dyes rather than natural ones are that:

- they are cheaper to produce
- they are easier to manufacture
- they produce a consistent colour every time
- a huge variety of colours can be made.

Synthetic dyes can now be produced so that they suit the properties of particular fibres and fabrics. Dyes are absorbed differently by different fibres, so it is important that a dye is selected with the fibre content in mind.

Affinity of dyes

The chemicals used to make dyes are unlike the chemicals found in fibres, so the two do not readily bond together – there is no **affinity** between them. To help create an affinity between the dye and the fibre, as well as to improve colourfastness, mordants are used in the industrial dyeing process.

Stages of dyeing

Dyeing can take place at several different stages of the production process, and this will depend on the fibres used and the items being made.

- **The fibre stage** – Dyeing the fibres themselves produces an end-product with a uniform colour because the dye has penetrated every fibre. Artificial fibres are dyed while they are still liquid and before they have been spun. Natural fibres are dyed loose in dye baths. A knitted jumper with a 'heather' effect is a good example of fibre dyeing, because the fibres are dyed different colours and then mixed together before the yarn is spun, giving the wool a random look.

- **The yarn stage** – This process is comparatively expensive because the yarn cannot be dyed in loose form the way fibres are, because it would become very tangled. Instead it is wound on to special containers. Although the dye is not distributed quite as evenly as it is in fibre dyeing, this is a good way to get clear stripe or check effects when different coloured yarns are woven or knitted.

- **The fabric stage** – This is a cost-effective method of dyeing, because fabric can be stored undyed, and dyed only when it is required. Stockings and tights are a good example of this, as the manufacturers can wait until they know which colours are selling well before dyeing takes place. This is sometimes referred to as piece dyeing, and is usually used only for plain-colour items. However, a patterned effect can be achieved if the fabric is woven or knitted using two or more different fibres and only one type of dyestuff. The different fibres have a different affinity for the dye, and so some areas will remain undyed. This is known as cross dyeing.

Sometimes dyeing takes place only when a whole garment has been made up. This is unusual unless it has a very simple design, because areas such as seams may be affected by the dye in a different way from the rest of the garment.

Environmental issues

Dyeing on an industrial scale is currently an important environmental issue. There are two main problems with dyeing.

First, the process requires vast quantities of water; and second, it results in unsightly and often toxic dye being discharged into the environment. Dye is not readily **biodegradeable**, and so new developments are being encouraged to find a different process that uses less water and does not do as much damage to the environment.

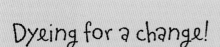

Clothes and accessories can be dyed easily and cheaply using synthetic dyes. A huge range of colours is available, and they produce consistent colours each time.

Dyeing for a change!

One of the most reliable and environmentally friendly methods of dyeing is pad-batch dyeing also known as the exhaustion method. The process can be used on cotton, rayon and blended fabrics.

The fabric is dyed, and the excess is squeezed out. The fabric is then stored and washed. This method offers advantages in waste reduction, reduced water consumption (up to 90%), reduced energy consumption (up to 75%), simplicity and speed.

Testing dyes

All coloured fabrics are expected to have a reasonable amount of colourfastness, although dyes are not necessarily fast with every type of fibre. Colourfastness can be divided into two areas:

- the change in the depth of the shade of colour
- the transfer of colour from a dyed fabric to another fabric (staining).

Why do dyed colours change?

Many things can affect fabric dyes and cause a change or staining of colour. These factors are referred to as 'agencies'. They can be introduced by the consumer in the process of washing or dry cleaning the item, or exposing it to light, perspiration or abrasion (rubbing). Or they can occur during the manufacturing process – for example, heat and moisture during pressing, atmospheric fumes in storage, and chemicals used in special finishing treatments.

Many dyestuffs, as well as fibres themselves, can be affected by the ultra-violet light in daylight which causes a chemical change in the composition of the dye. This change can create compounds which then speed up the process of deterioration in fibres – a process that is accelerated even further by washing the fabric. The change in colour brought about by light is usually referred to as 'fading', which means a loss of colour strength. If a fabric is likely to be exposed to light for long periods of time – e.g. curtains, beachwear, holiday clothes – then the dye selected should obviously have maximum light fastness.

Dye fastness

Fibres vary in their ability to hold dye. This can be tested in a laboratory by evaluating the colour change that occurs after the fibres have been washed. A sample of dyed fabric is washed in a washing machine with a multi-fibre test strip attached to it. This test strip consists of a piece of fabric divided into sections containing different types of fibre. So, there might be a section of wool fibres, a section of polyester fibres, a section of cotton fibres, and so on.

The fabric is washed at the correct setting for its type and then examined to see whether its colour has changed. The multi-fibre strip is studied to see whether any of the dye has transferred on to the fibres. The amount of colour change, or dye fastness, cannot be based on personal judgement, so a system known as 'grey scales' is used. The series of fibres are assessed using the

A multi-fibre test strip. This strip is used to assess the dye fastness of samples of dyed fabric.

grey scales measurement. It moves from no colour change seen, for which 'no change' is recorded, to total dye absorption, for which 'heavy staining' is recorded.

Dying results

If the test shows that the dye is not completely colourfast, a number of options are available. Firstly, the test could be repeated using a different machine wash setting, for example a cooler temperature. Or, if the dye did stain some of the other fibres the item could be labelled 'wash separately' or 'dry clean only'. Failing that, the fabric could be sent for re-dyeing or be totally rejected.

What makes a good dye?

To produce satisfactory results, a dye used for most textile fabrics needs to have the following properties:

- colourfastness
- light fastness
- perspiration fastness
- be insoluble in dry cleaning fluids (dry clean only)
- be unaffected by salt water and chlorine (swimwear)

The fabric has to be tested properly to ensure that the correct dye has been chosen for the fibre or fibres involved. There is a fast dye in most colours for every type of fibre.

Desirable fading

A textile company in Huddersfield called Nuance Ltd. are experimenting with dyes that have the effect of fading into one another. The dye in a single length of yarn changes while the yarn is being manufactured, producing perfect continuity rather than a series of breaks in colour. The company specialize in high-quality cashmere and cashmere/silk yarns, and have produced a range of knitwear using their new colour technique.

An example of dyes that can produce a faded effect. This new colour technique causes the dye in a single length of yarn to change gradually.

Inspired ideas

New products and textile items appear on the market every day. Perhaps this is not so surprising, given that the term 'textiles' covers a huge range of different products, from domestic to industrial. However, new ideas have to come from somewhere – and anyone involved in designing textiles, from GCSE students to professional designers, must be constantly on the lookout for **innovations** in textiles.

It is rare for someone to think of a unique idea without any prompting at all. When a need has been identified, textile designers are often given a **design brief**. This states the intended use of the product to be designed. Most **design ideas** are the solution to a particular problem, and it is not necessarily the person who has identified the problem who goes on to solve it. Ideas may also develop from discoveries that are made during experiments or research; this has certainly been the case with many new fibres and fabrics.

Specifications

Once a problem has been identified and a design brief written, a great deal of research and investigation is carried out to gather information about exactly what is needed. Its precise nature must be studied to ensure the need is fulfilled. This may involve talking to consumers, looking at similar existing products, and questioning experts about the technicalities of the problem. Research and investigation can take many months, even years, depending on the complexity of the idea to be developed.

If the results of the research indicate that the problem can be solved, financially as well as practically, then a design specification is produced. This contains the details of what the designer will require in order to develop the ideas further. It will include the function of the product, any cost limitations and types of materials needed, as well as considerations that are specific to the **consumer target group**. Armed with the design brief and design specification, the textile designer can start to generate ideas.

Inspiration for ideas

It would be impossible to list everything that could be used as a source of inspiration when designing. Ideas can develop from many different things as casual as glancing in a shop window or chatting to friends – so the most important thing is to be observant; you never know when your observations might come in useful!

However, ideas do sometimes need to be prompted, so designers often have to carry out research while looking for inspiration. Colour swatches, fabric samples, yarns, threads, accessories, and even items of jewellery or food can all help get the creative process happening. Inspiration may come through studying nature, art or music, or by reading books, newspapers or magazines. It is also essential to find out as much as possible about the consumer target group the product is aimed at – what influences them and what they like.

To capture the mood of a new product, a range of items are collected together on a mood board.

Trends in society

Just as fashion can be influenced by trends in modern society, so can all other areas of design. Natural fabrics and neutral tones are currently favoured, so textile designers are using these for carpets and other soft furnishings. When people in the public eye show a preference for a particular trend or image, this often becomes popular with the general public and designers need to be aware of this influence.

Mood boards

A **mood board** literally shows the 'mood' of a product. It might contain swatches of fabric, yarns, threads and so on, or even photographs and pictures – anything collected during the research that can be used to influence the design. A mood board is likely to indicate a colour scheme and will also reflect the feelings of the consumer target group. Working drawings (sketches) are also sometimes added to the board.

Design by nature

A collection of bags called the Parasite range has been designed using 'biomemetics'. This is the study of nature's way of adapting to its surroundings. The bags have a hard outer covering, imitating the protective shell of turtles, and straps that relate to spiders' webs!

Tie-dye

Tie-dye is a way of adding colour, and therefore pattern, to fabric. It is a **resist method** of dyeing. Other examples of this method include batik, adire, tritik, Japanese shibori, Malaysian plangi and silk painting using a gutta resist. The resist method simply means that something is resisting or stopping the dye from getting to some parts of the fabric. In the case of tie-dye knots, string, rubber bands, paper clips, and many other objects are used to resist the dye.

Tie and dye

Tie-dye is an old and very simple method of creating patterns. During the 1970s, tie-dyed clothes and bags were very popular and, like many aspects of seventies fashion, they reappeared in the 1990s. This also links with the nineties trend for natural methods and a natural look, because tie-dyeing is a traditional textiles hand craft, often produced with readily available resources, including natural dyes.

Tie-dye involves knotting or tying the fabric very tightly at regular or random points. The fabric is then dyed but the areas constricted by knots or string are unavailable to the dye. Once the fabric has been left in the dye for the appropriate length of time it is rinsed and dried. The result is an irregular combination of undyed and partially dyed shapes on a coloured background. Unlike printing, tie-dye does not produce precise patterns that can be repeated time and again, so tie-dye designs can be regarded as a truly unique decoration.

Creating colours

Two colours can be mixed together to produce a third colour (see page 5), and this is how different **colourways** are achieved in tie-dye. For example, if a sample of white fabric is tied randomly and dyed yellow it will result in white patterns on a background of yellow. Then, if that same fabric is tied in different places and dyed blue, the white areas will appear blue, the yellow areas will appear green and the areas tied for a second time may be yellow or white! If this sounds confusing, have a go and see the effect for yourself!

Creating effects

In addition to knotting or tying the fabric, different effects may be achieved in other ways. Perhaps the pattern most often associated with tie-dye is circles that radiate out at intervals from the centre of the fabric.

Tie-dye was a popular way of decorating clothes in the 1970s and 1990s. It is an example of resist dyeing.

This circling effect can be produced by lifting a square or circle of fabric from the centre with two fingers, creating a 'tube'. String or rubber bands are then tied around the fabric at intervals. Once dyed, circles of pattern appear where the fabric has been tied.

Other tie-dye effects include scrunching up the fabric by hand into a ball and tying it on the outside very tightly. Alternatively, the fabric can be folded into pleats which are then secured at intervals.

Extra effects

It is also possible to create different patterns by tying small pebbles or buttons in the fabric or trying out other methods of resisting the dye. For example, tritik is a technique that uses stitches and a non-absorbent thread to produce a pattern. Paper clips, bulldog clips, even staples, can be used when experimenting with unusual effects.

Hot and cold dye

A number of commercial dyes are now available for use with tie-dye or other crafts, or just to alter the colour of a textile item. Cold-water dyes are easy to use – you only need to add a dye fix and some salt. The amount of fabric that can be dyed with one packet or tin is written on the label. Using too little dye for the amount of fabric can result in an uneven colour. If you prepare too much dye you can store the excess in a screw-top plastic bottle and use it on another occasion. The bottle should be clearly labelled and kept well away from food.

Hot-water dyes work in a similar way to cold-water dyes, but as they work at a higher temperature they are not suitable for all fabrics or textile items. Machine dyes are useful when you want to dye a large quantity of fabric, because the dyeing takes place in the washing machine.

Tie-dye produces an endless variety of effects and is easy enough to be carried out at home.

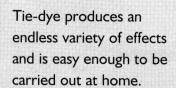

Batik

Batik is another example of the resist method of dyeing. The word 'batik' comes from Indonesia and means 'wax writing'. Although batik as a craft is practised mainly in Java and Indonesia, it is also popular in south-east India, Europe and parts of Africa, especially Nigeria.

Hot wax

Whereas tie-dye uses knots or string to resist the dye, batik uses hot wax. The benefit of melted wax is that it is absorbed into the fabric, hardening as it cools, and so prevents the dye from penetrating the fibres. The wax can be removed relatively easily after the dyeing has taken place.

The batik technique is often used on silk fabrics because they are naturally absorbent, although cotton and linen are also used. Many synthetic fabrics have poor absorbency, and don't hold hot wax or absorb cold-water dyes very well. Any new fabric being dyed should be washed first to remove possible finishes or dressings that it may have been treated with. Once immersed in the dye solution, the wax often cracks, giving batik its characteristic marbled effect.

Melting points

When wax is melted for batik its temperature should not rise above 137°C. Different types of wax have different melting points, but it is best to use a combination of 50% beeswax and 50% paraffin. Wax specifically designed for batik can be bought from craft shops and suppliers, and usually comes in particles, making it easy and quick to melt. It also means a small amount can be melted at a time, if necessary. In doing batik it is essential to control the temperature of the wax carefully and to follow safety precautions, as hot wax can cause serious burns.

Tools of the trade

For best results, batik should be done while the fabric is held taut in a frame. This stretched position helps the fibres absorb the wax and makes it easier to keep the fabric steady. It also keeps the fabric and wax off the work surface.

Traditionally the hot wax is applied to the fabric using a special tool called a *tjanting*. This handheld tool consists of a small metal bowl with a very thin spout. The hot wax is collected in the bowl and carefully applied to the fabric using the spout. This allows detailed and intricate designs to be created, and the metal bowl helps to keep the wax melted while working. Brushes may be used as an alternative to the *tjanting*, or when large areas need to be covered in wax. However, it is not as easy to apply wax with a brush because the wax cools and hardens more quickly.

Reverse batik is another alternative if a *tjanting* is not available. The framed fabric is covered in hot wax using a large brush. Once the wax has set, it can be scraped away with a sharp tool, following the pattern you want to create. When the dye is applied, it is accepted by the patterned areas of the fabric, which are free of wax.

A batik wall hanging that has been hand-crafted in Sri Lanka.

Cold dyes

Obviously only cold-water dyes can be used for batik, so the wax does not melt again. A dye fix is used to prevent the colour from running when the fabric is washed, or when the wax is removed if it is removed using water.

Different colour effects can be achieved by repeating the waxing and dyeing of a fabric several times. For example, part of a design could be applied in wax and the fabric dyed red. Then, more wax could be applied to protect areas of the design that are supposed to be red, and the fabric dyed blue. The resulting fabric would have patterns in red, blue and purple.

Removing wax

After the batik has been dyed and the fabric is completely dry, the wax has to be removed. It can be scraped off, but any that remains has to be removed using heat. This means either placing the fabric in boiling water, or else laying it between layers of absorbent paper and ironing over the top of it. The heat from the iron melts the wax, which is then absorbed by the paper.

Printing

There are various methods of applying colour to fabric that come under the heading 'printing'. Those that can be carried out at home or school are considered here.

Block printing

Block printing is one of the earliest forms of printing and, if done carefully, it can produce effective designs. Beginning with a block of wood, cut out a pattern on its surface to create a raised design. This must be done accurately as any marks in the raised part of the wood will be transferred to the fabric. Next, cover the design in paint, either by brushing it with paint or by dipping it into paint, so it is evenly coated, and then press the block down on to the fabric. Finally, lift the block off the fabric slowly and evenly. If another colour is required the first application of paint must be completely dry before the next one is added, and each colour uses a new block.

Screen printing

Unlike block printing, screen printing requires some specialist equipment. It is necessary to have a fine mesh screen and a squeegee which is used to spread the paint. Screen printing is time-consuming and, as a different screen is needed for every colour used, it can be expensive to do at home.

This method is useful for simple designs with specific areas of colour because the design is built up, one colour at a time. First, the design needs to be created in stencil form; so, for example, there might be one stencil for a flower stem and leaf (green), and one for the flower's petals (pink). The stencils are cut out of a thin sheet of card or plastic film which the dye cannot penetrate. The stem and leaf stencil is then placed inside the screen, which is laid on top of the fabric. Green paint (which

Students screen printing large areas of fabric.

holds the dye) is put at the top edge of the screen, and the squeegee is used to spread the paint evenly across the stencil. In the process the paint pushes through the gaps in the stencil. Once this is dry a different screen, containing pink paint and the flower stencil, is needed to complete the picture.

Stencil printing

It is thought that screen printing developed from the Japanese technique of stencilling. To stencil, cut the desired shape to be printed (usually a small shape that will be repeated) out of paper or card. Then apply the stencil paint with a brush or sponge, to colour those parts of the fabric that are exposed by the stencil. Once again this technique must be carried out with care, to avoid smudging the printed shape. Keep the fabric as taut as possible and hold the stencils firmly in place. When the paint is dry the stencils should be lifted slowly from the fabric.

Transfer printing

This method of printing literally transfers a design from one medium to another. Commercially produced transfers are available for use on fabric, or one can use transfer inks, pens, or crayons to produce a design, which is then transferred to the fabric. Transfers are created on special paper using **disperse dyes**.

Place the transfer, design-side down, on to the fabric and apply heat by ironing the back of the paper. This causes the dye to change from a solid to a gas, and soak into the fabric, where it returns to solid form. The dye is also made colourfast during this process. The only difficulty that can arise is remembering to create the design back to front!

Fabric pens can be used to add detail to designs, along with other techniques such as embroidery or quilting. Fabric crayons provide thicker lines and are useful for filling in larger spaces.

Fabric dyes and paints

Printing inks

Fabric crayons and pens

Marbling inks

Transfer drawing crayons

And finally...

Not strictly printing, but probably the simplest method of applying colour to a fabric at home, is to paint directly on to the fabric. This can be done using fabric paints, pens or crayons. You apply fabric paints with a brush, just as you would paint a picture. However, as fabric is involved it is important to practise the design beforehand to avoid making mistakes. The paint can also be applied using a sponge to create a textured effect, or the paints can be used when stencilling.

Textile project: Pill box hat

The following project involves making a pill box hat using one or more of the techniques you have read about in this book.

The fabric from which you choose to make your hat needs to be dyed first before you cut out the pattern shapes. Decide on the colour scheme you wish to have and the effect you wish to create. It may be worth looking at the section in this book on tie dye (pages 14 and 15) to give you some ideas.

What you will need

- Cotton fabric for the outer section of the hat. You will need 33 cm x 50 cm.
- Lining fabric 50 cm.
- Oddments of contrast fabrics for appliqué designs.
- Iron-on fusible webbing such as Vilene.
- Sewing thread, needle, pins, ruler, pencil, compass, pattern paper, scissors.
- Sewing machine.
- Dylon fabric dyes, salt, glass bowl, gloves, apron, tongs, elastic bands, buttons, cling film and paper towels.
- Microwave and heat proof gloves.
- Iron and ironing board.

Dying to get going

Dye the outer fabric first using your desired technique. Next prepare the dye by adding 2 tablespoons of dye powder and salt into the glass bowl, and then add 1 pint of cold water. Tie the fabric to create your chosen pattern using elastic bands, beads, buttons etc. Ensure the ties are tied very tightly so the dye cannot penetrate through.

Place the tied fabric into the dye mixture (dampen the fabric first). Make sure the fabric is fully submerged in the dye otherwise it will look patchy. Cover the bowl with a piece of cling film and pierce once, then place it in the microwave and heat on full power for 4 minutes.

Remove the bowl from the microwave using heatproof gloves, and carefully take off the film. Lift the fabric out of the bowl using the tongs. Squeeze out any excess dye and place the fabric onto a paper towel to cool and dry slightly. Once it is dry untie the elastic bands and other ties and spread out the fabric. Iron out the wrinkles and admire the effect!

Making it

Note: you should allow for a 1.5 cm seam allowance throughout.

1. To make the crown pattern, draw out a 20.3 cm diameter circle onto paper and cut it out. Measure and cut a paper hat band 70 cm x 8 cm. Pin the crown to the hat band and try it on for size, adjust to fit. Pin the pattern pieces onto the lining fabric and the outer fabric, and cut out one circle and one hat-band of each.

2. If you wish to add any appliqué designs, patchwork or fabric paint ideas to the hat, this should be completed now.

3. Once you have finished all your creative effects on the crown and hat-band, pin and tack (**tacking stitches** are large stitches that hold the fabric together and are removed after

machine sewing) the hat-band to the crown with the right sides of the fabric facing each other. Try this on and adjust if necessary. Machine sew the two ends of the band together and then sew the band on to the crown.

4. Repeat this process for the lining pieces. With the cap inside out and the right sides together, sew the lining around the bottom edge leaving a 6cm gap. Pull the inside of the hat through the gap until it is completely pulled to the right side. Then, push the lining up into the hat and over sew the gap closed. Press lightly along the bottom edge of the hat.

These hats have been decorated with embroidery.

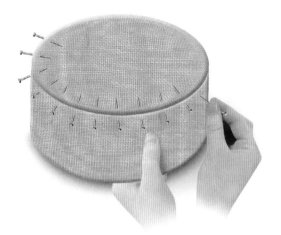

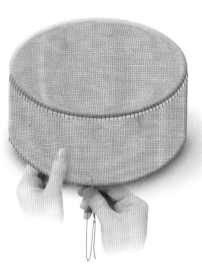

Alternatively...

You could use another very simple but effective way to create a bit of a splash on fabric by using a spray diffuser. You place one end of the diffuser in a pot of slightly watered down fabric paint. Then, as you blow air through the mouthpiece, the paint cascades out the other side. This is a useful tool to combine with stencils, producing a simple but effective design.

Industrial printing

Industrial fabric printing is based on traditional hand methods, but is obviously a much faster process. Vast quantities of fabric have to be produced for the mass production of textiles. The print on the fabric must also be precise in order to meet high standards of colour and pattern consistency. The three main types of industrial printing are screen printing, block and roller printing, and transfer printing.

Screen printing

Screen printing accounts for about 78% of all fabric printing in the UK. It uses the same principles as small-scale screen printing but is carried out using large machinery. Rotary screen printing is commonly used in industry because it allows the production to be continuous, making it more cost-effective. The screens are cylindrical and their circumference determines the size of the design repeat. A different colour, in the form of printing paste, is pumped into each cylinder and continuously squeezed through the fine mesh screen on to the fabric moving beneath. More than 300 metres of fabric per minute can be printed using this method!

An alternative method is flat-bed screen printing, where the fabric is held flat on a surface using a special adhesive. The screen is held above the fabric by a conveyor which automatically moves along the fabric, one screen width at a time. As the screen is lowered on to the fabric, printing paste is applied to the screen and a squeegee or roller forces it through the mesh. The screen is then lifted and moved on to the next section of fabric.

Industrial screen printing.

Block and roller

The traditional method of printing with blocks is modified in industry with the use of rollers. The rollers have a copper surface from which a design is cut. A separate roller is used for each colour. The printing paste is fed into the rollers and then pressed on to the fabric which is passing below. A design can be built up by having a series of rollers containing different colours, arranged around a drum. The design is complete when the fabric has passed under all the rollers on the drum. Roller printing does not produce detailed designs as well as other methods, and it is also relatively slow and expensive.

Transfer printing

Transfer printing is most successful on synthetic fabrics such as polyester. It requires the application of heat and the use of special dyes. Initially the design is printed on to paper using disperse dyes. Then the paper is placed on the fabric, printed-side down. The fabric is subjected to a high temperature by means of a heated **calender** which causes the dye to change into a gas. Once in the form of a gas, the pigments of dye are not attracted to the paper but attach themselves instead to the fibres of the fabric, where they return to their solid state.

Transfer printing is a relatively cheap process. It is also more environmentally friendly than other printing methods because it does not require water or produce any pollutants. It also produces a fabric that is colourfast straight away. However, on the negative side, it is more difficult to know precisely what shade

of colour will be produced by transfer printing. As high temperatures are involved, it can be used only with a limited range of fabrics.

Some other ways to print on textiles

- **Resist printing** – using the resist principle of tie-dye or batik, this method involves applying a resist to the fabric to prevent the dye penetrating certain areas.
  The resist is actually printed on, so once the fabric has been dyed and the resist removed, the printed area is free from colour.

- **Discharge printing** – this is a bit like printing in reverse! The fabric is dyed first and then overprinted with a paste containing a chemical that will destroy (or discharge) the dye. The areas that have been overprinted show a different colour from the background of the fabric.

- **Flock printing** – this method is frequently used on furnishings and wallpapers. It involves applying an adhesive to the fabric and then adding cut fibre snippets to provide a textured effect.

Applying patterns

One way to apply colour and pattern to a fabric is by attaching other fabrics to its surface. This is the basis for the technique known as appliqué. Appliqué is the application of one piece of fabric to another by means of stitching. It is a textile craft with a long history, and it is still popular in many countries including India, Russia, Pakistan, Central and South America. Appliqué is functional as well as decorative, because by adding layers of fabric a garment or textile item can be made more durable (hard-wearing). It is also useful for patching up fabric that has become worn or ripped.

Appliqué has **aesthetic** as well as functional qualities. For example, quilts, wall hangings, pictures and cushions can all be given the unique 'collage look' that is achieved through appliqué. Pictures can be created by cutting out shapes in fabric and sewing them on to a background material, or **abstract** designs can be created from scraps of fabric and coloured threads.

Planning appliqué

First of all, it is necessary to have a design for the appliqué (unless the design is to be created as you work, in which case it is good to think about a theme or a colour scheme). The design may be something that can be copied from a book, magazine or painting, or it could be designed specifically for the appliqué. It is important to remember that each area of the design has to be cut out in fabric and stitched on to a background, so it should not be too small or intricate.

When planning a piece of appliqué work it is important to consider the types of fabrics being used. For example, they might be all cotton, or all of natural origin. If they need to be easy-care fabrics, synthetic fibres might be the best choice. On the other hand, designs often need lots of different textures and colours which can be produced only by choosing a wide variety of fabric types. Whichever fabrics are chosen, they should be cut so their **weft** and **warp** threads run in the same direction as those of the background material. The background material should also be sturdy enough to hold layers of fabric.

Another important consideration in choosing fabrics is whether or not they fray. As appliqué involves stitching around the edges, the edges of a fabric that frays badly need to be turned under before stitching. A fabric like **felt** does not fray so it can be a useful choice.

Hand appliqué

All appliqué was traditionally done by hand. Although this is a time-consuming method, it is still very popular, particularly with smaller textile items such as **motifs** for sweatshirts.

Before cutting out the shapes to be used, apply a fine, iron-on **interfacing** to provide added strength. Then, starting with the background shapes first, and working up to those on the surface, pin or tack the design in place. When sewing the fabrics it is best to use a herringbone stitch if they fray, or for turned or unturned edges use slip stitch or hem stitches. Threads of contrasting colours can add to the design.

An appliqué design. The technique of appliqué is an excellent way to embellish textile items. Beads, sequins and even tiny mirrors can be part of the design.

Machine appliqué

Fraying is not such an issue with machine-stitching because satin stitch completely covers the edges of the fabric. Alternatively use a very close zig-zag stitch, or a stretch stitch if the fabric is stretchy. It is important that the shapes be tacked in position before stitching, or they are likely to move, even if held by pins. Also it is worth practising stitching around corners and curves before embarking on an appliqué design.

Special effects

Like so many textile techniques, appliqué can be combined with other methods of decorating fabrics. For example, padded appliqué can add texture and a raised effect to an otherwise flat design. By cutting out some wadding, slightly smaller than the shape that is to be padded, and then placing it under the fabric shape and stitching as before, a particular area can be emphasized. This can be further enhanced with beads, sequins, buttons or even tassels.

Patchwork patterns

Patchwork is the traditional craft of joining pieces of fabric to form a larger unit of patterned fabric. In North America the craft dates back to the settlers of the early seventeenth century. They did not have much money, and used the technique as a way of creating a comfortable home using every last scrap of fabric.

Patchwork shapes

The shapes in a patchwork are usually straight-sided – squares, diamonds, triangles, pentagons, hexagons etc. This is because they have to fit together without any gaps. The main characteristic of patchwork is the interesting effect produced by the fabric pieces after they have been joined.

A one-shape patchwork is the easiest type to make because all the pieces are the same size and shape. The pieces may all be the same colour, but when several colours are used together, it creates a more interesting design.

All other patchwork is known as block-unit patchwork. This is because the fabric pieces are first joined into a block that is regarded as the basic shape, and that shape is then repeated throughout the patchwork. Even random patchwork designs can be of a block type, because patterns that use the same range of fabrics are created in blocks, e.g. squares, and then all the blocks (squares) are joined together.

Patchwork by hand

Patchwork is time-consuming when it is done by hand, as every piece of fabric must be carefully joined to the next so the stitches are invisible on the right side.

Machine patchwork

Patchwork can be produced a lot more quickly if it is done by machine, and with the current interest in recycling, patchwork has once again become popular. Today, patchwork is evident in fashion items such as jeans and jackets. The simplest type of machine patchwork to produce is based on squares. Once a series of squares has been joined to form strips, these can be sewn together in one go, along the edge. However, it doesn't take much alteration of shape, size, colour and combination of fabric to produce an endless number of designs.

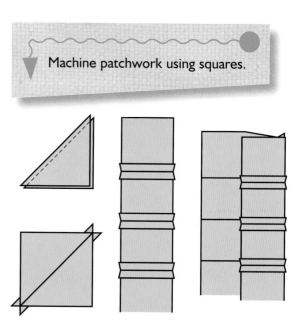

Machine patchwork using squares.

Recycling Textiles

TRAID - Textile Recycling for Aid and International Development, is a charity committed to protecting the environment and reducing world poverty by recycling clothing and shoes. The collection of textiles for reuse and recycling provides both environmental and economic benefits:

• Reduction in the need for landfill space

- Reduction of pressure on virgin resources
- Reduction of pollution and energy use, as fibres do not have to be transported from abroad.

Unwanted clothes that are donated are hand sorted or redesigned and reconstructed to make new recycled garments, and sold through fashion forward charity shops.

Through its strong branding, TRAID has gained a reputation for being innovative and edgy, appealing to a young, fashionable and environmentally conscious audience.

TRAID Remade was set up in 2000 as a direct response to the abundance of waste created by the fashion industry; TRAID Remade provides an ethical alternative in fashion on the high street. From recycling banks to catwalk, from celebrity **clients** to television, TRAID Remade has transformed the image of second-hand clothing and is now heralded as the leading fashion recycling charity.

The creation of the TRAID Remade range is developed using a variety of techniques. Many are traditional craft techniques like appliqué, crochet and patchwork, but used to create very contemporary clothing. Often a garment starts at the pattern cutting stage, where either a length of vintage fabric is cut to the designer's requirements or a garment is taken apart, re-cut and reconstructed to make something completely new. Sections of vintage fabrics are used to create appliqués on structured and modern shapes. This gives the garment its character. The use of graphics and printing techniques are endless in their possibilities and are used in striking contrast with the traditional florals of vintage fabrics.

3D patchwork

Patchwork is an excellent medium for producing three-dimensional (3D) textile items. Consider the soft toy balls given to babies: they are often made from patches of felt fabric, usually in bright primary colours. The shapes are cut out of flat fabric, but when joined together they form a 3D ball, like segments in an orange.

TRAID Remade collections offer a wide range of styles from hard edge images made from leather appliqués on distressed t-shirts through to intricate crochet features.

Old textiles can be recycled to make beautiful patchwork clothes like this.

Quilting

A quilted fabric is an example of a layered fabric; a layer of woven or knitted fabric on each side of a layer of **wadding**. The wadding is held in place with stitching, often in a decorative pattern. Quilted fabric is used where warmth is needed – for example, jackets, body warmers, table mats and bedding.

Insulating properties

Quilting a fabric provides insulation because air is trapped both within the wadding and between the layers of fabric. Wadding tends to be made from a washable polyester and is designed to trap air within its structure. The light texture of wadding means it is not very durable, so the outer layers of fabric prevent it from deteriorating. The stitching used in quilting must be kept to a minimum, otherwise areas of thin fabric are created and the insulating effect is lost.

Decorative effects

Quilting is more than just a functional fabric, because the stitching used to hold the layers of fabric in place can be applied decoratively. Also, as quilting involves padded areas of fabric, it can provide depth and texture to textile items. Quilting can be combined with other techniques such as patchwork, to improve the aesthetic value of the product.

Quilting techniques

Like all traditional textile crafts, quilting was carried out by hand; but the process can now be done easily and quickly using a sewing machine. Quilting does require careful preparation to ensure that the stitched design is accurate and that the layers of fabric do not move during construction. Frames are used in the manufacture of industrial quilts, or if large pieces of material are involved. The quilting design is marked on after the three layers of fabric have been assembled and set into the frame.

To quilt on a small scale, secure the layers of fabric by stitching a cross through the centre of the fabric (see the diagram). This also acts as a guide for the design. The design can then be marked on the outer layer of fabric using **tailor's chalk** or tacking stitches. The lines must be measured very accurately to avoid a distorted pattern. If the pattern requires straight lines and the outer fabric is fairly thin, you can place graph or squared paper behind it and use it as a guide (before sewing the three layers together).

Layers of fabric are secured by stitching a cross through the centre.

Quilting stitches

The thread used for quilting can be a colour that contrasts with the fabric, but in this case it is even more crucial that the stitched lines are sewn straight, as a contrasting colour will make them more obvious. Most domestic sewing machines have a quilting 'foot' which helps to act as a guide. This is an adjustable crossbar which runs along the previous line of stitching to ensure the next line is parallel to it. The foot also has upturned 'toes', so the thick wadding can pass freely under them.

It is possible to create a completely random quilted effect by stitching without a pattern, developing a unique design as you stitch.

Italian quilting

Italian quilting produces a fabric with a raised design and requires a padding yarn rather than wadding. A layer of fabric and interfacing are tacked together and the design is machine stitched on top using two parallel lines of stitching. The gap between the stitching provides a space for the padding yarn. With the reverse of the fabric uppermost, the padding yarn is threaded between the stitching, creating a raised design. The interfacing is cut at intervals so the needle and yarn can be pulled through and reinserted (see the diagram).

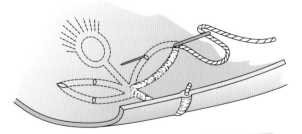

Puff quilting

Padding yarn can also be used to achieve an effect known as puff quilting. This is where the edges of something like a pocket are given a padded look by machine stitching several parallel lines with spaces between them. The padding yarn is then threaded through the gaps and drawn through to the end. The reverse fabric does not need cutting with this technique, and the effect is to emphasize the edge of a garment or textile item.

Trapunto quilting

Trapunto originated in Italy in the early 16th century. It is a whole cloth quilting technique which produces a raised surface on the quilt. Trapunto patterns can be threaded with a soft yarn or cording or machine stitched. The rounder shapes are stuffed with small amounts of kapok or synthetic toy stuffing, inserted from a small slit made in the backing fabric. After the shapes are stuffed, the slit is stitched closed.

Sewing techniques

Apart from quilting, other methods of enhancing fabric by means of surface decoration include pintucks and piping.

Pintucks

Pintucks are folds of fabric held in place with stitches, and they range from a couple of tucks, for example at the waistband of trousers, to a whole series of tiny tucks. Pintucks can serve a purpose as well as being decorative, because they give shape and fullness to an area of fabric where it is required.

Functional pintucks are used at the waistband of skirts, trousers and shorts to allow for the fact that people usually narrow at the waist, so unless the waistband is elasticated, more fabric will be needed below the waistline. Pintucks are also used at the shoulder or yoke of women's dresses and tops to provide fullness for the bust.

Decorative tucks are used on many garments, particularly shirts. Very formal dinner shirts have rows of pintucks running down the front, each side of the buttons and sometimes around the neck instead of a collar. Pintucks are perhaps less obvious in household items, yet many sofas have a frill of tucks around the bottom edge. Duvets and cushions are often effectively decorated with pintucks which provide a surface interest without adding more in the way of colour.

Making pintucks

Pintucks are very easy to do, although when they are small and there are many of them it is important to measure and sew accurately. Commercial patterns often indicate pintucks using lines, and these markings have to be

Tucks are often used at the front of trousers to provide fullness and shape.

transferred to the fabric. The fabric is then folded from one line to the other and secured, first by ironing, then by pinning and sewing. The tucks may be stitched across the top or stitched down their length.

When designing textile items with pintucks it is important to consider the direction of the tucks – for example, pintucks at the waistband are usually folded towards the centre. Extra fabric has to be allowed for tucks, and items containing a lot of pintucks are usually more expensive because of the added fabric and labour.

Piping

Piping is a technique that is likely to be associated with furnishings, as the edges of sofas, chairs, car seats and cushions are often piped. Piping is the addition of a cord covered in fabric along the edge of a textile item. The cord can vary in thickness, and the fabric may match or contrast with the main material.

Piping provides a neat finish and added visual interest.

Piped products can be relatively expensive, as they require more fabric and more labour than unpiped versions. However, piping provides a neat finish and added visual interest.

On the bias

The fabric used to cover piping cord must be sufficiently flexible to encase the cord and to bend around corners where necessary. It should not be too bulky and, although it contrasts with the rest of the fabric, it should have similiar care instructions. In order for the fabric to be sufficiently flexible it must be cut on the bias. The bias of a fabric runs diagonally across the fabric's weave. If a strip of ordinary woven fabric is cut along the weft or warp it will not have any stretch, but if a strip of the same fabric is cut diagonally it will have a small amount of stretch. Special bias binding can be purchased and used to cover piping cord.

Piping method

In order to add piping to an item, you need sufficient lengths of biased fabric. If they have to be joined then this must be done beforehand (sewing diagonally with the bias). The fabric must be wide enough to cover the cord, with some excess to act as a seam. The cord should be long enough to pipe the entire area, if possible. First, wrap the cord in the fabric, right side showing, and secure with tacking stitches. Then place the prepared piping in the middle of two pieces of fabric, right sides facing. The piping must face inwards while the extra fabric acting as a seam touches the outer edge of the fabric. When all three layers are secure, they have to be machine stitched close to the piping. On turning the fabric round the right way, the piping will appear between the two layers of fabric.

Manipulating fabric

Gathering is another example of a decorative technique that also serves a purpose. Like pintucks, gathers can give fullness to an area and make fabric curve – for example, around the top edge of a sleeve, so that the sleeve fits into the armhole. Gathering may be purely decorative and used to create a frill on a garment or item such as a bag. It can be seen on clothes and on soft furnishings.

Gathering principles

The principle of gathering is the same whether it is carried out by hand or by machine. Two rows of even stitching are applied to the fabric edge that needs to be gathered. Each row of stitching is secured at one end only, but at opposite ends to one another. This allows the fabric to be gathered from both edges, ensuring an even distribution of fabric. Once the gathered fabric has been attached in the appropriate place, the gathering stitches are removed.

Hand-stitching gathers is time-consuming and care has to be taken to ensure the stitches are the same size, otherwise the gathers will be uneven. Machined gather stitches are usually larger than normal machine stitches, so that the fabric is relatively easy to gather. However, the stitches can snap quite easily, so gathering should not be done too quickly!

Smocking

Smocking is a decorative form of gathering. It has traditionally been sewn by hand on aprons, nightwear, and children's and babies clothes, but through the ages the smocked 'look' has come and gone with fashion

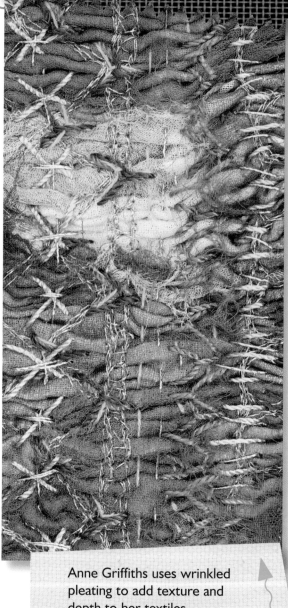

Anne Griffiths uses wrinkled pleating to add texture and depth to her textiles.

trends. The recent 'peasant style' fashion uses smocking for blouses and dresses. Smocking is still popular for babywear and children's clothes because it gives children more freedom of movement, and space for bulky nappies. Young children have not yet developed a waistline, so clothes that are smocked at the chest provide room for their tummies. In addition, smocking can look very attractive and is often used in the design of Christening gowns.

Pleating

A pleat is a fold in the fabric held in position by stitching at the top or side. They can provide fullness and enable a fabric to flow. There are four kinds of pleats, flat pleats, projecting pleats, accordion pleats and wrinkled pleating.

Flat pleats – these are parallel folds lifted from the surface of the fabric and laid down to the side. They include knife pleats, box pleats and set in pleats, all are secured with a stitch at the top and released below.

Projecting pleats – these are folds lifted from the surface of the fabric and arranged so that they stand out from the fabric itself. They include pinch pleats, organ pleats and cartridge pleats.

Accordion pleats – these are made by folding fabric alternately in and out, creating projecting pleats. This is the kind of pleating used for smocking and can be performed by hand, or mechanically on a smocking pleater.

Wrinkled pleating – this consists of irregular ridges made by securing damp, bunched fabric and leaving it to dry. It includes broomstick pleating where the fabric is rolled around a cylinder, when unwrapped; the folds all lie in one direction. Contortion pleating is where the fabric is twisted into a rope, coiled and knotted. When dry the folds lie in all directions.

Fabric manipulation using heat and stitch

Diana Rhie is a designer who uses heat to manipulate and change the surface of a fabric. Diana uses a heat gun to create her surfaces, directing the flame for one second over a section of flat fabric. This causes that area to suddenly shrink up, creating gathers from the surrounding fabric. This technique creates volume and texture without taking away from the intricate surface already prominent on the garment. She then hand and machine stitches into the layers of fabric stiffened to plastic by the heat manipulations creating pleats, gathers and pin tucks which give her designs such definition.

For this beautiful and unusual fabric, Anne Griffiths used indigo dye and mineral salts.

Fabric manipulation using stitch

Anne Griffiths is a textile artist and teacher who works with sheer fabrics, different dyes and a variety of stitches to produce beautiful fabrics and textiles. She mainly embroiders using a machine to create and manipulate images and patterns.

Embroidery

There are few forms of decoration that have had such a long-lasting appeal as embroidery. It is startling to realize that embroidery was carried out as long ago as 5000 BCE. Today, it is still a highly fashionable way of decorating clothes and accessories.

Decorative stitches

Embroidery stitches are used in one of two ways: to create an outline or to fill in a shape or design. Of course, both types can be used together – for example, stem stitch may form an outline while satin stitch fills the space in the middle. Filling stitches can completely hide the fabric, or a lacy effect can be achieved by using open stitches such as feather stitch.

'Embroidery' can be defined as the application of coloured threads on to fabric in order to enhance the fabric's appearance. Different threads provide different textures, and patterns can range from tiny delicate designs to large areas filled in with stitching. Most types of fabric can be used for embroidery, as long as the weave is even and the fabric will not be distorted by the sewing. Threads are made from silk, cotton, wool, synthetic fibres, metallic fibres, even plastic. Intricate stitches look the best and are easier to create using fine threads.

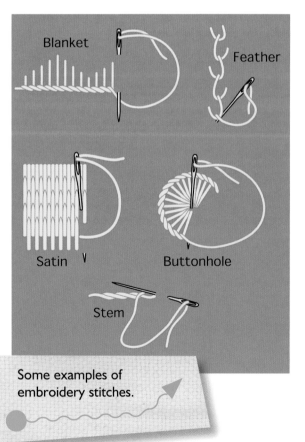

Some examples of embroidery stitches.

Blanket · Feather · Satin · Buttonhole · Stem

To do hand embroidery you usually need an embroidery frame, also known as a *tambour*. It consists of two wooden loops, one inside the other, with a fastening on the outside loop. The fabric is placed over the smaller loop, and then the larger loop is put over the top and fastened down tightly. This ensures the fabric remains taut and even while the stitches are sewn. Embroidery needles tend to be thicker than sewing needles, with longer, wider eyes.

Industrial embroidery

The textile industry uses special embroidery machines, often computer controlled, to produce embroidered items. Hand embroidery is a time-consuming process so it is not practical for large-scale production. Industrial one-off items (known as '**job production**') may be hand embroidered, but these are much more expensive because of the cost of labour and the fact that the item is unique.

Examples of a piece of
embellished cloth produced
by Jennie Zipperer.

By using software that has been programmed
with designs, and machines that stitch the
designs very quickly, embroidered items can be
produced at prices affordable to most people.

Machine embroidery

Small-scale machine embroidery can be done
at home or school using sewing machines that
have a choice of embroidery stitches available.
Some people own computerized sewing
machines, which work in the same way as
conventional sewing machines but have the
ability to embroider stitches and designs that
have been programmed into them.
If attached to a scanner, a sketched design
can be automatically stitched and even stored
for repeated use. Some machines can be
connected to computers so the screen is
used for designing.

Thread painting

Embroidery may be thought of as a way of
painting a picture on fabric using threads. The
art of thread painting takes this idea further.
You need an ordinary domestic sewing
machine, as well as fabric fixed in a tambour,
but in this instance the foot of the machine is
removed. This enables you to move the fabric
in any direction and so 'paint' an embroidered
picture. Obviously, you can stop to use a new
colour of thread and to change the type of
stitch. This technique requires a lot of practice.
You have to be in total control of the machine
while you sew. However, it does enable you
to produce items that are unique.

Jennie Zipperer is a textile designer who creates
beautiful embellished fabrics. She uses layers
of silk to give the fabric depth and colour and
produce a multi-dimensional feel. She also
adds embellishments, like beads and threads to
create artwork that is beautiful and unique.

Fancy clothes

To 'embellish' something means to enhance, decorate or improve it. For example, someone might embellish a story by exaggerating some of the detail to make it more exciting for the listener. Fabric can also be embellished to make it more exciting, by using techniques such as embroidery or the addition of details like buttons.

Appliqué and embroidery are techniques of fabric embellishment that we have seen already. Other ideas for embellishment include sequins, tassels, buttons, bows, knots, net, lace, zips, motifs, badges, beads, even jewellery. Embellishment adds interest and originality to products but it can also be used to jazz-up something that is old, faded or worn.

Clothes talk

Historically clothes have played a major part in revealing a person's status. Not just the fabric, but the style and detail of the embellishment have told us a great deal about a person's wealth and their position in society. For poor members of society, clothes could be little more than a form of protection, but the upper classes have used the appearance of their clothes to 'show off' their status.

Throughout the ages there have been some elaborate and highly decorated fashions which must have taken many months to make and were probably very uncomfortable to wear!

This 'language' of clothing is less evident today, although uniforms are still used to identify roles and occupations. To many people the cut of a suit can say a lot about how much the wearer has paid for it.

Queen Elizabeth I in 1592. Her dress is a shining example of the taste of the Elizabethan court: gold and pearl decorations, and the colour combination of coral red, black and white.

School uniforms not only identify the school a child belongs to, but they help to make all children feel equal, without the competition of wearing the trendiest garment.

An example of highly decorated clothes in relatively recent times is punk fashion. During the 1970s punks used safety pins and chains as a means of embellishment for their clothes (and often themselves!) Their clothes were usually black and enhanced with rips and tears. The **non-conformist** look was complete with hair formed into spikes, high on the head and dyed unexpected shades such as green or purple.

Dramatic costumes

Probably the only places to see elaborate historical clothes today are in period dramas and at the theatre. Period costumes for television have to be specially made and they must be as accurate as possible in every detail. It would be no good making a Georgian dress with a zip fastening! Just as the actors must study the period in order to act and behave in the correct manner, so costume designers must consider the fabrics, styles and methods of decoration and replicate (copy) them as closely as they can.

Theatrical clothes

People who are designing clothes for the theatre have additional considerations. The actors must be clearly recognizable from a distance and their clothes must not clash with the scenery, or with each other. The choice of fabric may have to be richer in some cases or more fine and flowing in others. The colours may need to be bolder and brighter than normal in order to achieve the correct effect. Rather than having a few simple decorations, a garment may need many brightly sparkling glass beads or sequins that catch the theatre lights and add to the magical atmosphere.

Extra embellishment

Trendy embellishment

Weddings, parties, theatre trips, clubs, restaurant meals and ceremonies, all provide an excuse to get dressed up. The clothes someone chooses to wear when socializing and relaxing can say a lot about the type of person they are, and the fashions they follow. Here are a few examples of different looks and how they use embellishment.

- ### The biker
  Never really out of fashion – leather jackets; trousers and boots, studded with metal; plenty of chunky zips. Leather belts and arm cuffs displaying a skull and cross-bones often complete the look.

- ### Eastern
  Gold bangles and beauty spots are a must. Fabric is either embroidered with gold or metal threads, or golden coloured designs are printed on afterwards. Sequins are an essential embellishment.

- ### Country and Western
  This one has a clear American feel, with lots of bright colours and embroidered jackets. Hats are important, as well as tassels.

- ### Casual
  Even those who prefer to feel comfortable and look casual whatever the occasion may be able to boast an embellishment. The most casual of clothes, the t-shirt, can be adorned with splashes of appliquéed colour or even a false pocket that is purely decorative.

A beautiful embroidered bodice. Both the dress and shoes have been embellished for a special occasion.

- ## Sporty
  Sport and fashion have become linked in recent years. Although most sportswear would not be practical with any kind of embellishment – apart from the brand logo that is often embroidered on – for some it is essential. Gymnastics, ballet and ballroom dancing, for example, all require a degree of adornment.

It's in the bag!

The latest trend is for more embellishment on fashion bags than ever before. Bags have been embellished with butterflies, edelweiss, feathers, motor bike straps, stabbed with decorative applied brooches and finished with chunky short chain shoulder straps.

Evening bags of gold, silver or gunmetal have been stitched over in a patchwork of metallic woven braids. The braids composed of Tyrolean, Ikat or Indian traditional designs, have roses, geometric images and kaleidoscopic elements adorning them. Silk foulard, Pucci style pattern print handbags for evening with short beaded shoulder straps and finished with bead tassels compliment the vintage look. Round hard cases like vanity bags decorated in spots, stripes and in strong solid colours that make the item part of the outfit also appeared as a bucket bag version.

The layered look

The 21st century has seen the layered look gain popularity, where different textures and a more sombre palette play against each other and are combined with interesting shapes. The deep triple belts, a string of beads or extra jewellery, Oliver Twist schoolboy caps, big knitted rib beanie hats or packable hats are all features of the new look.

Opulence

The new fashion trends take in several themes including Napoleonic and costume drama styling and the continuance of modern, but smart ladylike looks. Opulent baroque brocades, with shimmering golds and metallics take inspiration from the imperial formal courts, and elements from the designer mixed with rich luscious extravagant fabrics, lavish stitching and 3D gold ornament embellishment.

Fur and fur trims

Hot on the heels of the opulent look is fur. It is now used in new ways to create whole garments from shrugs to capes to coats. Fur trim details are very important. Smartly tailored and volume coats are highlighted with fur collars and cuffs.

Fake fur is now of a high standard and if your ethos is to avoid wearing fur then you have plenty of choice to choose fake.

There are abundant faux fur trim on jackets, gloves and bags. Burberry trench coats have fur trims including collars, cuffs or hems and sometimes part of a whole skirt of the trench coat is made from fur. Many designers are also using deep bands of fur hems on dresses and on skirts.

Sparkling decoration

Fashion is a big dictator in terms of what people wear and how they wear it, but technology plays an ever increasing role too. The current trend is for clothes made from fabrics that fit where they touch and are comfortable and versatile; Lycra® is a good example of this. Another fashion trend is for sparkle and decoration.

Brody International – a case study

In order to combine the stretch of Lycra® fabrics with the sparkle of sequins, Brody International, Europe's only sequin manufacturer, have developed a sequin with stretch. High-**tenacity** Lycra® is attached to the sequins, making a sequin-covered garment more comfortable to wear. A new system known as 'slinging' makes it possible for two high-tenacity yarns to be knitted into a straight 'trim', and this provides a base for the sequins. Previous methods have used static cotton threads, which limits the end-use of sequins on stretch fabrics. Now, it is easier to knit braids, trims and finished garments, and this means sequins may well appear in areas of the textile market where they have previously been excluded – for example, in lingerie and swimwear.

Now it is possible to have a sequin trim that stretches with the fabric, making clothes more comfortable.

Sequin quality

When it comes to **quality control**, the latest method of sequin manufacture has sorted that out, too. Obviously it is important that the amount of stretch is controlled and always remains constant, and this is achieved by using a purpose-built tension meter. The meter also prevents an unequal balance of the two yarns as they are knitted, which would otherwise result in the trim being twisted.

Embellishing the 21st century

The trend for embellished textile items seems set to continue well into the 21st century. Brody International are proof of the increased demand, because they had to put on extra shifts in their factories during the build-up to the millennium and their overseas markets had growth rates of over 200%!

All items used to embellish fabric, not just sequins, must match the trends in fashion, so it is now possible to find buttons with transparent effects that give a 'not quite there' feel to the fastening. Poly-vinyl-chloride (PVC) has been produced with special tortoiseshell or shot silk effects, and it is also possible to have PVC net. Zips are now even more functional as well as decorative (when they can be seen, that is!), because they come in waterproof and invisible varieties. Lace is no longer just lacy; it can also be manufactured with a rib, making it more versatile in the production of clothing.

Embellished fabric

Of course, with all these advances in technology it is not surprising that some fabrics simply will not need to be embellished because they will be part of the embellishment themselves. Fabrics can be created with a laminated plastic film embossed with tiny lenses. If such a fabric were used to make curtains, for example, then as people moved around the room the colour of the curtains would change as the lenses **refracted** different areas of pattern in the fabric.

Another example of a modern fabric with 'in-built' embellishment is a 'burnt-out' material. In this process a chemical is added to the fabric before it is printed with a pattern, then it is baked at a high temperature. This causes the pattern to burn away, leaving a fabric with a lacy appearance.

A fabric with a ready-made, highly textured surface is achieved using acids. These are added to the fabric, which initially becomes elongated before being left with a 'puckered' look.

This effect was created by screen printing chemicals in a grid pattern. The synthetic fabric used is shot polyamide organza, which blisters in the process.

Fashion phrases

Fashion forecasters often use rather weird and wonderful terminology to describe trends. Here are some phrases used to describe fashions of the future: 'cool and delicate', 'biological and vegetal' (meaning 'from vegetation'), 'elegant and witty' and 'full of enlightenment'.

Household decorations

Home decoration became big business during the 1990s and the trend is set to continue. Do-it-yourself or DIY stores are in every retail park, and many shops that once only sold clothes, such as Laura Ashley and Next, have moved into interior decoration. The interest in home improvement in Britain can also be judged by the popularity of television programmes such as 'Changing Rooms'.

Perhaps not everyone is brave enough to have their neighbours decorate an entire room for them, but most people are keen to have a go themselves. And this is not just an adult interest; many teenagers and students want to express their personality and individuality by decorating their bedroom to suit their taste.

Embellishing a room

Giving a room a 'make-over' does not necessarily mean re-decorating the whole room and buying entirely new accessories. Although a lick of paint can brighten things up, this can also be achieved much more quickly with a homemade rug, a stencilled wall or a wall hanging. Embellishing a room can be easy if you think of detail rather than the room as a whole. Door handles can transform a chest of drawers in the way new buttons can liven up an old jacket. Separate handles can be found in many DIY stores, department stores and craft shops. They can have novelty value or they can give a piece of furniture a more up-market feel.

Trends in interiors

Texture is a word to memorise in the 21st century, because it touches every feature of design; on walls, in fabrics, in wood finishes and in flooring concepts. Furnishing fabrics are dominated by textures and weaves that focus on the in-built beauty of natural fibres. Fabrics with metal woven into them, tones and thread work, embroidery and quilting are all making a comeback. Prints are back in favour but the motifs are eclectic and the colours very bold. Polka dots and stripes refuse to go out of fashion. Windows are no longer bare. Colour and embellishment complement modern styles. The emphasis is on creating a fusion between the old world style and the modern look. Metal, leather, and suede are all being used with linen, cotton and silks. Handwork and detailing bring elegance to the earlier minimalist styles and embroidery, printing and ethnic styles have re-created their space in design.

Creating an effect

Whether designing a room or an item to go in a room, one has to consider the overall effect. Different colours can create different effects, such as 'cool' blue and 'warm' gold, but the effects of a particular fabric or shape of an item are less obvious. For example, a rather serious, business-like image is created by a sofa that has a strong, smooth, fitted cotton cover, whereas a sofa with loose fitting covers, pleated at the bottom edge, creates a cosy, more homely effect. Windows with blinds can look more formal than curtains, and they can also give the illusion of more space.

Designing interiors at any level requires planning, preferably after doing some research. As we have seen, inspiration for ideas can come from all sorts of places, and a mood board is extremely useful for gathering thoughts and ideas and looking at the overall effect. If you have chosen a particular colour scheme, then collect items to suit that colour.

Interesting themes can come from all sorts of places, so it is a good idea to collect items for inspiration.

Ergonomics

Ergonomics is the study of the relationship between people and their environment. It is involved in the design of all products. Highly complex ergonomic research may be necessary. For example, it is no good designing a totally original and attractive dining chair if it is too low for the person sitting to reach the table comfortably, or if it makes their back ache after five minutes. By studying the size and height of people and objects, designers for the mass market can ensure that their products match the 'average' person, if not everyone. One-off items, on the other hand, can be totally 'tailor-made'.

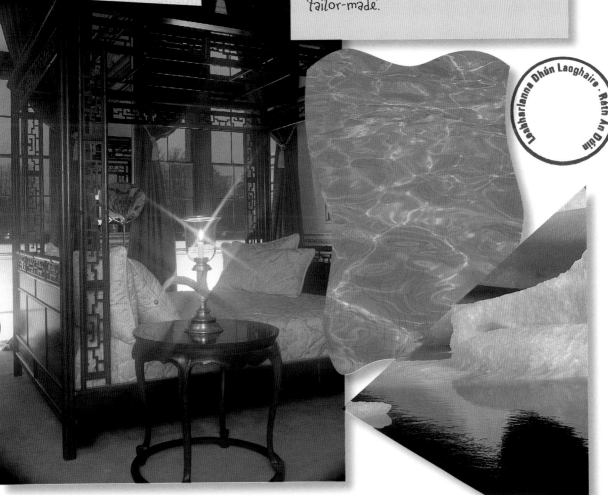

Leabharlanna Dhún Laoghaire · Ráth An Dúin

Resources

Books

The following books are useful for students studying GCSE Design and Technology: Textiles Technology:

GCSE Textiles Technology for OCR Carey Clarkson, Jayne March and Joy Palmer *(student book and teacher resource file)*	Heinemann 2002
Revise for OCR GCSE Textiles Technology Carey Clarkson and Maria James	Heinemann 2003
GCSE Design and Technology for AQA *Textiles Technology* Rose Sinclair and Sue Morgan – student book Carey Clarkson and Justine Simmons – teacher resource file	Heinemann 2006

The following books are useful for more detailed information on embellishment techniques:

Appliqué Pauline Brown	Merehurst Limited 1990
Techno Textiles 1 and Techno Textiles 2 Sarah Braddock Clarke and Maria O'Mahony	Thames and Hudson 2006

I.C.T.

www.brody.co.uk
Sequin and textile manufacturer

www.craftscouncil.org.uk/exhib.htm
Provides details of forthcoming arts and crafts events throughout the country

www.textile-toolkit.org.uk
Includes news, competitions, details of events and a chat forum for students. There is also a CD-ROM available for use as a teaching aid for GCSE textiles

www.worldtextile.com
Publishes a variety of textile-related journals

www.embellishmentcloth.com
Information about Jennie Zipperer a designer who works with layered fabric, paint and thread.

Places to visit

Colour Museum
PO Box 244
Perkin House
Providence Street
Bradford
West Yorkshire BD1 2PW
(Tel no: 01274 390955)

*The museum consists of two galleries,
'The World of Colour' and 'Colour and Textiles'.
You can learn about colour and how it is
perceived and find out about dyeing and textile
printing from ancient Egypt to the present day.*

The Design Museum
28 Shad Thames
London SE1 2YD
*Exhibits focus on design evolution in the
20th century.*

Victoria and Albert Museum
Cromwell Road
South Kensington
London, SW7 2RL
*Textile exhibitions and Crafts
Council shop*

Syon Park, West London
(Tel no: 020 8560 0881)
*Arts and crafts events and shows throughout the
year.*

Embroiderers' Guild
Apartment 41
Hampton Court Palace
East Molesey
Surrey KT8 9AU
(Tel no: 020 8943 1229)
*The collection is international and includes
embroidered and stitched textiles dating from
the 1600s to the present day.*

Contacts

The Crafts Council
44a Pentonville Road
London N1 9BY
(Tel no: 020 7278 7700)
*Provides up-to-date information about art and
crafts exhibitions and shows; also produces a
magazine called Crafts, available on subscription*

Tech Soft UK Ltd
Falcon House
Royal Welsh Avenue
Bodelwydden
Denbighshire
LL18 5TQ
(Tel no: 01745 535007)
www.techsoftuk.co.uk

Vicky Emery (Education co-ordinator)
Emtex Limited
Designer Forum Studio
69-73 Lower Parliament Street
Nottingham NG1 3BB
*Information about smart and modern materials
and industrial processes*

Glossary

abstract not looking like anything in particular

aesthetic relates to the beauty of something rather than other considerations, such as usefulness (function)

affinity where things have a close similarity

biodegradable able to be broken down (decomposed) by bacteria

calender a machine which smoothes paper or cloth by passing it between two rollers

client a person or company who has commissioned (requested the services of) a designer to solve a design problem

collage a picture made up of pieces of different material, including paper, cloth, photographs etc.

colourfast term used to describe a fabric from which dye will not wash out or rub off

colourways the same design shown in different colours

consumer target group the group of consumers being targeted for a product because they are the ones most likely to buy it; e.g. elderly, teenagers, sports women etc.

design brief a short statement about the intended use of the product to be designed

design ideas sketches to illustrate ideas which fulfill the design brief; they may be annotated (labelled) and coloured

disperse dyes dyes that are chemically attracted to fibres rather than water

dye a substance added to textiles in order to give it colour; natural and synthetic dyes may be used

dyestuffs another name for dyes

embellishment special decorations or adornments added to clothing and accessories to make them more attractive or interesting

felt the matting (or felting) of hair fibres if they are washed at too high a temperature, or too vigorously

hue another word for colour

innovations something totally new and original

interfacing fine material used to support certain areas of garments and textile items

job production production of unique items; they usually involve a lot of time and skill and are relatively expensive to buy; sometimes called 'one-off' production

mood board a board covered with pictures, sketches, swatches etc. that is used to create a mood or feeling about a product to be designed; often used when talking to the target consumer group. Also known as a theme board

mordant a chemical that can 'fix' the dye so it will not wash out or fade

motif a repeated image or theme in an artistic work

non-conformist someone who does not wish to follow the common trends in society

pad-batch dyeing a method of dyeing. The fabric is padded with a solution of dye. It is then stored on rolls or in boxes to prevent the water evaporating. This is cost effective, simple, quick, flexible and it reduces waste and water use.

quality control a way of checking the quality of a product during or at the end of its production

refracted bend in a ray of light when it hits glass or water

resist method a method of dyeing (batik, for example) that uses something to prevent (resist) the dye reaching the fabric

shade a darker variant of a colour. Produced when black is added to the colour.

synthetic produced chemically, not naturally e.g. polyester

tack hold together using temporary stitches

tacking stitches stitches used to hold a fabric in place while it is being sewn; a cheap thread is used.

tailor's chalk used to mark out fabric for cutting; often flat with a sharp edge for marking fine lines; easily removed with a brush

tenacity the strength of a fibre

tint a lighter variant of a colour. Produced when white is added to the colour.

wadding lightweight but bulky fabric, often made in polyester, used to pad or stuff textile items; has a loose structure, so can trap air when needed for heat insulation; soft enough for toys or padding areas of appliqué

warp the vertical threads in a woven fabric

weft the horizontal threads in a woven fabric

yarn single strand of fibres spun together

Index